NATURE CLUB

ANIMAL BABIES

JOYCE POPE

Illustrated by
ANDREW ALOOF

Troll Associates

Nature Club Notes

Though you may not know it, you are a member of a special club called the Nature Club. To be a member you just have to be interested in living things and want to know more about them.

Members of the Nature Club respect all living things. They look at and observe plants and animals, but do not collect or kill them. If you take a magnifying glass or a bug box with you when you go out, you will be able to see the details of even tiny plants, animals, or fossils. Also, you should always take a notebook and pencil so that you can make a drawing of anything you don't know. Don't say "But I can't draw" – even a simple sketch can help you identify your discovery later on. There are many books that can help you name the specimens you have found and tell you something about them.

Your bag should also contain a waterproof jacket and something to eat. It is silly to get cold, wet, or hungry when you go out. Always tell your parents or a responsible adult where you are going and what time you are coming back.

Do not try to touch baby animals. They may look sweet, but they are often fragile, and easily hurt. Most mother animals do their best to protect their young. They do not know that you do not mean to harm them, and they will risk their lives trying to drive you away. If you watch from a distance, the family may become used to you and eventually let you come closer.

Library of Congress Cataloging-in-Publication Data

Pope, Joyce.
    Animal babies / by Joyce Pope ; illustrated by Andrew Aloof.
       p.   cm. — (Nature club)
    Includes index.
    Summary: Discusses different kinds of animal babies, how they are
born, fed, and educated, and where they live.
    ISBN 0-8167-2773-2 (lib. bdg.)   ISBN 0-8167-2774-0 (pbk.)
    1. Animals—Infancy—Juvenile literature. [1. Animals—Infancy.]
I. Aloof, Andrew, ill. II. Title. III. Series.
QL763.P66 1994
591.3'9—dc20   91-45381

Published by Troll Associates

Copyright © 1994 by Eagle Books

All rights reserved. No part of this book may be reproduced or utilized in any form or by any means, electronic or mechanical, including photocopying, recording or by any storage and retrieval system, without permission in writing from the Publisher.

Designed by Cooper Wilson, London
Edited by Kate Woodhouse

Printed in the U.S.A.

10 9 8 7 6 5 4 3 2 1

Contents

Introduction

One of the most important things that living creatures do is produce a family. Like human parents, all other animals do their best to give their children a good start in life. Since most animals are small and short-lived, they cannot all care for their young for very long. Often they just try to make sure that they have enough food.

Bigger animals such as mammals and birds generally live longer, and usually provide more care for their young. Sometimes both parents tend the family and bring food while the babies are helpless. Many kinds of animals would not recognize their fathers, for only their mothers care for them. In a few cases, particularly certain kinds of cichlid fish, the fathers protect the babies. Some fathers even nourish the babies before birth.

▲ At birth, the young dolphin weighs about one quarter as much as its mother and is able to swim with her right away.

◄ These bear cubs were only about the size of guinea pigs when they were born.

4

The babies of mammals tend to look like their parents. A baby elephant is clearly an elephant, and it is obvious that a lamb will grow up to be a sheep, just as the human baby is like its parents. But many kinds of small animals, mostly creatures without backbones, have young that are born or hatched as *larvae*. Who would guess that a tadpole is a baby of a frog, or that a caterpillar comes from an egg laid by a butterfly? These babies are very different from their parents because they lead a different kind of life while they are growing.

▼ The blue butterfly dies soon after laying its eggs. Caterpillars hatch from the eggs. They grow and change before they become butterflies in the adult stage of their lives.

▶ Elephants have only one baby at a time. The young grow up in a herd of females.

Babies from Eggs

Most living creatures hatch from eggs. Some of the biggest eggs are laid by ostriches, and the smallest by some kinds of tiny sea creatures. Inside an egg is the *embryo*, or growing baby animal, and a little food for it as it develops.

In almost all cases there is a tough shell around the egg. The shell acts as an armor to protect the little creature inside. On land, it prevents the embryo from drying up. Some insects lay eggs because their *grubs* have to wait several months before they hatch. They are safe inside the eggshell for that time.

When birds and reptiles hatch, the eggshell's job is finished. For many insects, the eggshell is the first meal for the tiny grubs, who then start to look for other food.

◄ The male midwife toad gathers the eggs laid by his mate around his body to protect them against enemies. He stays in moist places so that the eggs do not dry up.

◄ Many insects lay their eggs near their food source so their insect grubs, like these caterpillars, can eat the right sort of food when they hatch. They will die if they cannot find the right sort of leaves.

Almost all fish lay eggs. A few kinds protect their young, as do some frogs and toads. Many reptiles, like crocodiles, look after their eggs. Some snakes and lizards keep their eggs inside their bodies until they are ready to hatch. Once they have hatched, the babies have to fend for themselves.

Birds' eggs must be kept warm and *incubated*. When the baby birds hatch, they are fed and cared for by their parents. Only two kinds of mammals lay eggs: the echidna, or spiny anteater from Australia and New Guinea, and the platypus, which lives only in Australia.

▼ The thrush makes a nest of mud and grass in which her eggs and chicks will be safe. Once hatched, the babies grow quickly and leave the nest forever by the time they are three weeks old.

Family Life

One of the great differences between human beings and other animals is that most human mothers usually have only one baby at a time. Many other mammals and birds have several babies at once. This means that humans often have older or younger brothers and sisters, while other mammal and bird families grow up with brothers and sisters of the same age. Most animals without backbones produce large numbers of young at one time. But, apart from the social insects (termites, ants, and some bees and wasps), they have no family life.

Another difference is that we grow up very slowly. Most animals grow up very fast. A fox cub born in the spring is an adult by winter, and has its own family the next year.

▼ Young raccoons born in the spring are able to live on their own by winter.

8

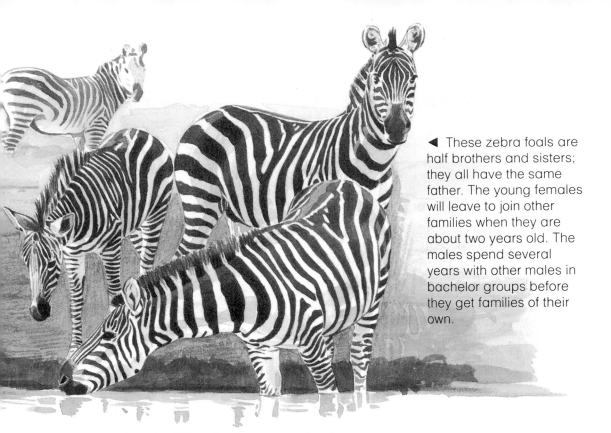

◀ These zebra foals are half brothers and sisters; they all have the same father. The young females will leave to join other families when they are about two years old. The males spend several years with other males in bachelor groups before they get families of their own.

Some animals, like elephants and zebras, live in family groups, so a new baby has older brothers and sisters around. They do not have much to do with each other, for there are usually several babies of about the same age that play together.

There are animals, like chimpanzees and beavers, where the mother may have a new baby before the last one is fully independent. She will have to give most of her attention to the new baby, but often the older one helps her to watch over it and groom it. Some kinds of birds, like gallinules, do the same. They are easy to watch, and you can see that the babies of the first brood help to feed and look after their younger brothers and sisters.

▼ Ducklings can run and swim before they are three days old. By the time they are two months old, they will have feathers and be able to fly.

How Many Babies?

Some animals have large families, while others have only one baby at a time. There are many reasons for this but, with warm-blooded creatures in general, the larger the animal, the smaller its family. It is extremely rare for whales, elephants, or large hoofed animals to have twins. On the other hand, some small mammals may have ten or more babies in a single *litter*, and may have several litters each year.

One reason large animals have small families is that most of them are unable to make a safe home in which helpless babies could be born. The baby has to be protected inside its mother's body until it is well developed. Baby whales can swim from the moment they are born. Smaller animals can easily make secure nurseries for their large families. The babies are helpless at birth, but they are able to grow in safety in the den.

▶ Giraffes have only one baby at a time. Though the young giraffe starts to nibble leaves when it is only a few days old, it drinks its mother's milk until it is about a year old.

10

▶ The Virginia opossum may have twenty or more young in a single litter.

▼ Snowy owls lay their eggs over several days, so all the chicks don't hatch at the same time.

There is no point in an animal giving birth to babies that cannot be reared because there is not enough food or shelter. Even so, many young animals die before they grow up. Some kinds of animals, like wild dogs and wolves, are able to limit the number of babies born. It is only the *dominant* female in a pack who gives birth, so all the cubs stand a fairly good chance of surviving. Others, such as snowy owls, have large families when there is plenty to eat and only a small number of young when food is scarce.

11

Feeding Babies

Young animals often need food which is different from their parents' food. Baby birds, which are often larger than their parents by the time they leave the nest, need to be fed on the most nourishing food. The adults may eat nothing but seeds, but they feed their young on insects and grubs. This is why you should be careful about the kind of food that you put out for birds in the summertime. If little birds are fed on bread, they will not grow properly and may die.

▲ Baby mammals, including humans, feed on their mother's milk. But, unlike most animals, humans are able to digest milk during their adult lives. The milk of other mammals, particularly cows, is an important part of our diet.

◄ Baby thrushes need large amounts of food. When they leave the nest, less than three weeks after hatching, they are almost the same size as their parents.

All young mammals are fed on milk from their mothers in the early part of their lives. The milk contains water, fats, sugars, and proteins, but the amount of each is different for each animal. The milk of most small mammals, such as mice, is low in fat but high in sugar. The milk of whales and seals may be over half fat.

Baby mammals are fed on milk for different lengths of time. Most small animals feed for only a few weeks, but larger ones may be fed by their mother's milk for two or more years. Eventually young animals change to an adult diet. Once this has happened, their digestive systems alter. They no longer need milk, and in many cases they are unable to digest it.

▼ Young deer may begin to nibble plants when they are about a week old, but they continue to drink their mother's milk for about ten months.

Growing and Learning

As an animal grows up, it changes in size and perhaps in color. Equally important, it also changes in behavior. Some of the changes in behavior are *innate*, or built into the growing process. As a caterpillar changes into a butterfly, for instance, its behavior alters automatically. Other changes are the result of learning about the world around them.

One of the first things a mammal or bird learns is what it is. Mammals learn the smell of their mother and brothers and sisters, perhaps even before they can see. Birds learn what they are as soon as they open their eyes. This is called *imprinting*. It is possible to imprint a creature on something other than its own kind. This sometimes happens with baby birds that are rescued after falling from their nest. Usually they think they are humans, or sometimes a dog. They may not recognize themselves as birds even when they are grown-up.

▲ Fox cubs are cared for by both parents, who bring them food and playthings. By playing, the cubs learn many of the skills that they will need when they grow up. They first leave the nursery den when they are about four weeks old.

▶ When this crow was very young, he fell from his nest and was rescued by a human family. He became imprinted on them, and never learned to be a bird. Each spring he would court one of the members of the family, bringing her presents such as worms, which he would have offered to a mate in the wild.

Mammals are playful when they are young. Even calm creatures like sheep leap and play king of the hill when they are lambs. But play has a purpose: young animals learn through play. Bear and lion cubs discover how to make a kill or defend themselves by play fighting. Young mammals also learn by following and copying their parents. Foxes educate their cubs by bringing squirrels or moles to the den. The little foxes pounce and shake and learn to make a kill while they are still quite young.

▼ In spring, lambs leap and play in the fields. They copy the behavior of adult sheep, which fight for mates in the breeding season.

Animal Nurseries

Most animals care only for their own young. Often a lost baby will be driven away by another female. This is because most creatures can only manage to rear their own families. If they were to take in orphans, it is possible that none of the babies would survive.

Lions live in groups, or prides, where it is likely that the females are sisters or cousins. Each year they have cubs at about the same time, and in the big family any female will feed any cub. Even if a cub's mother is away hunting, it will always have food and protection.

A pack of wild dogs or wolves normally produces only one litter of pups each year. These are usually born to the dominant female. Only she can give them milk, but the other members of the pack help her to rear them.

▲ Young king penguins are often left alone for several days while their parents are at sea collecting food. They huddle together in a big group, or crèche, for there is safety in numbers.

▼ Lion cubs are well looked after by all the females in the group, or pride, in which they live. A young cub begins to fend for itself as it learns to become an expert hunter.

They care for the cubs and bring them solid
food when they are old enough to eat it. In this
way all members of the pack act as parents.
Because there are a few babies getting a lot of
care, a high proportion of them survives.

When some animals, such as the king
penguin, search for food they leave their
babies in a nursery group, or *crèche*. The
chicks are safer because there are so many of
them. Packed together, they are less likely to
be attacked by enemies such as skuas. When
the parents return, they call their chick. The
chick knows its parents' voices and follows
them to be fed.

▼ African hunting dogs
live in family groups, or
packs. The puppies are
looked after by all the
adults in the pack. From
an early age, the young
pups learn to take their
place as part of the pack.

Babies in Pouches

Baby mammals start their lives inside their mother's body, where they are protected and provided with food. Most of them are quite large when they are born. But there are exceptions. There are two kinds of egg-laying mammals and many kinds of pouched mammals, or *marsupials*. Most of these live in Australasia, but some are found in parts of North and South America.

▼ Wallabies are small relatives of the kangaroos. The tiny baby, or joey, grows in its mother's pouch for nearly nine months.

▲ Koalas are often called koala bears. But they are not bears. they are marsupials. which are pouched mammals. A baby koala weighs less than one-fiftieth of an ounce (½ g) at birth. It grows in its mother's pouch for seven months and may stay with her until it is over a year old.

▶ The quoll is sometimes called an Australian native cat. It is not a true cat; it is a pouched mammal.

The babies of pouched animals are born after a very short time of growth inside their mother. They are tiny – the biggest is only about three-quarters of an inch (2 cm) long and the smallest about the size of a grain of rice. They have no fur, are blind, and cannot hear. But most of them have well-developed forelimbs. They use these to scrabble through the hair of their mothers' belly. They eventually reach a pocket or pouch in her fur and there they stay.

Once inside the pouch, a young marsupial finds its mother's milk. The baby grows, but more slowly than other sorts of mammals. After about 5 months, a baby red kangaroo looks out of the pouch for the first time. It hops out for a few minutes when it is about 6½ months old and, at about 8 months old, it is strong enough to leave permanently. Even then it continues to take milk from its mother for another three months.

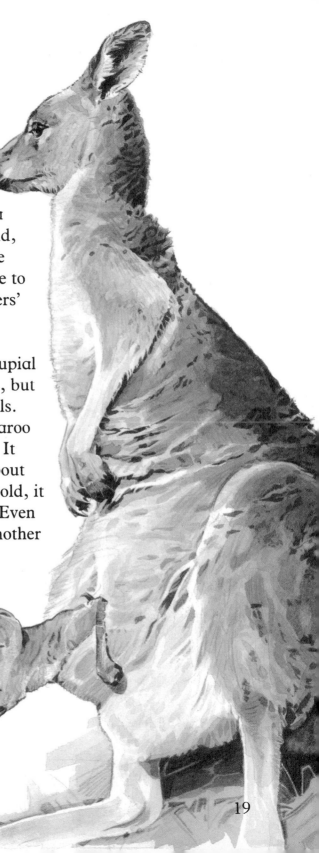

► The red kangaroo is the largest of the marsupials. At birth, the joey is about the size of a butter-bean and weighs one-quarter of an ounce (less than 1 g). The joey lives in its mother's pouch for about eight months, by which time it weighs almost nine pounds (over 4 kg).

19

Babies in Dens

Foxes, mice, bears, and shrews are some of the many kinds of animals born in a den. A den is usually a hole dug underground in a dry place, but it may be made in a variety of sheltered spots.

Den babies are usually part of a large family, and are born at an early stage of their growth. Often den babies are born tiny, without fur, blind, and helpless. This does not matter, as they are safely hidden from enemies and bad weather, and are kept warm in a bed of dry grass and leaves. The babies lie by their mother when they feed. It is hard work for her to produce enough milk for them. She must leave them occasionally to search for food for herself.

After a few days, the young ones start to grow fur. Then their eyes and ears open and they begin to explore, first their home and then the area outside. Many den animals are *nocturnal* and only venture out at night. The

▲ Baby pigs are born in the winter, while their mother is resting in a secure den.

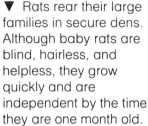

▼ Rats rear their large families in secure dens. Although baby rats are blind, hairless, and helpless, they grow quickly and are independent by the time they are one month old.

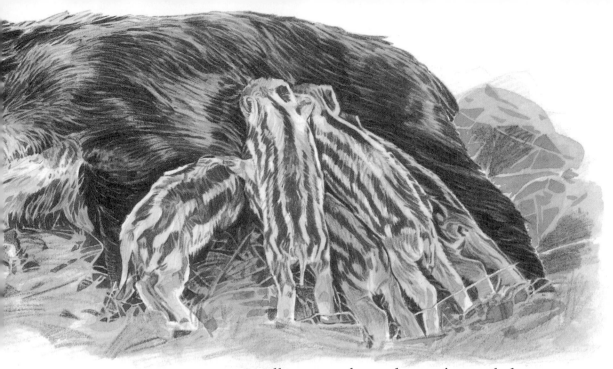

small mammals, such as mice and shrews, grow up and leave the den very quickly. The babies of meat-eating mammals often stay with their mother for much longer. A brown bear cub might follow its mother for two or three years.

▼ This ermine is busy moving her family to a new den, because she is afraid that an enemy has found her nursery.

21

Babies on the Plains

Large hoofed mammals that live in herds on grassy plains, such as bison or antelope, cannot make dens to protect their babies. These babies are born in the open and face the same dangers as their parents. They have fur, their eyes are open, and they can hear well. They are able to stand up minutes after birth and to follow their mother shortly afterward.

It would not be possible for the females to produce a large family of such big babies. Normally only one is born at a time. At first the baby stays very close to its mother. Soon it is introduced to the rest of the herd where there are usually playmates of the same age, as most females give birth within a few days of each other.

Whenever possible, meat eaters attack animals that cannot protect themselves, so they kill many newborn plant feeders. Plains mammals grow and gain strength very quickly.

▲ A zebra foal stays close by its mother for a few days, then plays with the other youngsters in its family group.

They are able to run with the adults to escape an attacker when they are only one week old. The whole herd is alert to danger and this helps to protect the babies.

Plains babies often begin to nibble plants when they are only a few weeks old, but their mothers give them milk for much longer, sometimes for over a year.

▲ A baby African elephant is protected by the adult females in the herd. A female elephant calf usually remains with the group her whole life. Young males leave when they are about thirteen years old.

▼ A baby bison can run about three hours after it is born, and is carefully guarded by its mother. As they grow up, the males move away to lead more solitary lives.

Babies in the Trees

Trees give safety to many small creatures that climb and jump and hide among the leaves. An oak tree is said to have about 300 different kinds of creatures that depend on it. Most of these are insects. When tree-living birds and mammals have a family, they often make a den in a hollow branch, though they sometimes build a nest where no enemies can reach them.

Most small birds make nests in trees to hide and protect their eggs and babies. Some of the most elaborate nests are made by weaverbirds. Some of them make huge nurseries for the whole flock, while others build nests with a long entrance tunnel, which may be to protect the eggs and babies from snakes.

▶ Gibbons swing and leap about the treetops in the forests of Southeast Asia. Newborn babies have to cling tightly to their mother's fur.

▼ The colugo is a gliding animal. Sometimes a mother makes a hammock of her flying membrane so she can carry her young with her.

▲ Some baby pangolins sleep in a hollow, high in a tree.

The young of tree-living birds leave their nests when they are able to fly. But many forest mammals carry their babies with them as they search for food. They are able to protect their young at all times, so it does not matter if an enemy finds the nursery. Some, like pangolins or sloths, are slow moving. Even so, the babies have to hang on very tightly because a fall could kill them.

A baby monkey or ape hangs onto the underside of its mother, but later rides on her back. Sometimes the father helps; some male gibbons take over most of the care of the children once they are a year old. Gorillas, chimpanzees and orang-utans make nests in the trees. The heavy males never climb very high, but the females and young rest on springy, mattress-like platforms as much as 65 feet (20 m) above the ground.

Sea Babies

The babies of almost all air-breathing sea creatures are born on land. Baby birds and reptiles that hatch from eggs would drown if they hatched in the sea, so however helpless the parents may be out of the water, they must go ashore for the sake of their young. Turtles struggle ashore at night and bury their eggs in the sand. Penguins and shearwaters, which are most comfortable in the sea, have to risk the dangers of land to rear their young. Seals and sea lions must find remote beaches to give birth to their pups.

There are exceptions. Some sea snakes keep their eggs inside them, and they hatch in the water. Sea otters are usually born in the water. Whales always are, because they cannot survive out of it. These babies are born tail first, unlike most other mammals, and have to get to the surface quickly to take their first breath.

▼ Wandering albatrosses lay a single egg which takes over two months to hatch. The parents feed their chick on partially digested food and oil from their stomachs. Nine months pass before the young bird can fly.

▲ Unlike land mammals, baby whales and dolphins are born tail first. The baby is pushed to the surface so that it can take its first breath of air.

▼ Manatees live and give birth to their young in warm shallow waters. The babies stay with their mother and feed on her milk for over a year.

All mother sea mammals produce milk that is very rich in fat, which helps their babies grow quickly. A young elephant seal, the biggest of seals, puts on about 55 pounds (25 kg) a day and is soon ready to go to sea. Most whales give birth in warm waters and return to colder regions where there is plenty of food. The babies stay close by their mothers, since they are fed by them during the *migration*.

27

Leaving Home

Although many small creatures are on their own from the moment they hatch, baby mammals and birds are dependent on their parents and do not move far from their mothers. As they grow older, they may remain close to their parents, for often this is how they learn about the world around them. The time young animals stay with their parents varies. Small animals generally become independent more quickly than larger ones. But eventually the babies strike out on their own.

This is necessary because as they become adults they trespass on their parents' living space and food resources. They may have to travel a long way before they can find a place to settle where they will, in time, rear their own families. But before this they must face many dangers. They have to find food without their parents' help and discover the things that are harmful to them.

▲ Goslings are able to feed themselves very soon after they hatch. In spite of this, family groups stay together even after the young are able to fly. This is probably because the young learn from their parents during their annual migration.

▼ Male fox cubs, born in the spring, leave their family group at the end of the summer. They sometimes wander into towns or neighborhoods, looking for food.

The exception to this is among social mammals like elephants, zebras, wolves, and chimpanzees. The young tend to stay with their mother until she has another baby. They may help to look after the new baby, but they stay as part of the *extended family*. They may leave eventually, but not for several years. Although they are no longer dependent on their mother, they stay friends. Chimpanzee mothers and their grown-up children, for example, are seen together more often than unrelated chimpanzees.

▼ Chimpanzee mothers often keep in touch with their older children and rely on them to help look after the new babies. In a party of chimps, mothers and grown-up offspring often feed together.

Glossary

crèche a group of young animals that stay together for safety while their parents are away finding food. There are usually other adults which protect the young in a general way.

dominant the leader of a group of animals. Sometimes the males and females each have their own leaders.

embryo a partly developed animal, before it is born or hatched.

extended family a group that contains a number of related animals besides parents and their offspring. Aunts, uncles, cousins, and more distant relatives may be included.

grub the young of an insect that does not look like its parents. A caterpillar is the grub of a butterfly or moth. Grubs go through a period of pupation during which they change to their adult form.

imprinting learning process by which animals learn from their parents what they are. In some cases, animals learn behavior from adults other than their parents.

incubate to keep eggs warm until they hatch. The embryos in the eggs develop during this time.

innate behavior that does not have to be learned. It is sometimes called "instinct."

larva (plural **larvae**) the young of an insect that does not look like its parent. A caterpillar is the larva of a butterfly or moth. Bees, flies, and beetles are all insects that produce larvae.

litter brothers and sisters all born at the same time. We talk about a litter of fox or lion cubs, for instance.

marsupial a mammal whose young are born after a very short period of development inside the mother's body. They continue their growth in a pouch on their mother's belly, where they are fed on milk. Most marsupials are found in Australia and New Guinea. A few come from South America and one, the Virginia opossum, is found in North America.

migration the movement, on a regular basis, of all or a large part of a population of animals from one area of the world to another. Some migration journeys are quite short but many are very long. They are made by many sorts of animals, including some insects, fish, birds, and mammals.

nocturnal an animal that is active at night.

pride a group of lions that live together. There may be as many as 30 lions in one pride, including one to five adult males, several lionesses (female lions), and their cubs.

Index